Your Herb Garden

by Anthony Lyman-Dixon
Illustrations by Tessa Lovatt-Smith

Contents

Through the book:

20 favourite herbs   (in alphabetical order)

Information boxes

SGC BOOKS

Basil

Half-hardy annual that needs warm and sunny conditions to grow to its full 30cm height. It seldom does well outside in Britain and suffers badly from slugs and caterpillars. Nevertheless it is such an excellent herb to cook with, it is worth making an effort by growing it under a garden cloche, or keeping it on the kitchen window sill. Can be watered during the day (unusually for herbs). *Basil* is an essential in Italian cooking and many Eastern recipes. Main constituent of **Pesto sauce** and goes well with tomatoes. Many varieties are available; sow seeds inside, in late spring.

1. Basil
(Ocimum basilicum)

1. First thoughts

For many people their first introduction to herbs was when they were given gripe water as a baby. Gripe water contains *dill*, a herb noted for its efficacy against digestive upsets, and perhaps it is that first soothing taste that has remained in the nation's subconscious to stimulate the phenomenal interest in herbs today.

Because herbs are inextricably bound up with two of mankind's major preoccupations - his health and his food - they exercise an irresistible fascination over people, even those who would otherwise rarely give their gardens a second thought.

Tussie Mussies.
Tussie Mussies are bunches of prettily arranged fragrant herbs pressed to the nose to repel malignant vapours (hence nose gays). They were originally in much demand by judges fearing infection by the criminals they were trying. In these egalitarian days, tussie mussies are commonly met with as attractive button holes. The Queen however still appoints a tussie mussie maker by Royal Warrant.

Herbs are deeply rooted in man's history, being used long before chemical pesticides and fertilisers, and so are relatively bug-resistant and easy to grow, unlike some modern vegetables. They therefore have a special appeal to organic gardeners and vegetarians and it is not surprising that for many young couples the first priority in their new garden is the establishment of a herb bed.

Garden centres now stock as many as eighty different kinds of herbs and seeing a full display for the first time can be somewhat unnerving to the inexperienced gardener. Actually, most herbs are very user-friendly, but it follows that what suits one variety will not necessarily suit others. It can be very discouraging when half your new purchases wither up only to be told by a helpful neighbour that your dead favourites *grow like weeds* in her garden. **20 favourite herbs** are highlighted throughout the book to help you choose.

This book also includes some **planting designs,** but they are no more than suggestions and should not be followed slavishly. A planting scheme is an expression of an author's personal taste and circumstances. You may be allergic to some herbs recommended, dislike the smell of others and be appalled by the suggested colour combinations, not to mention possessing a garden shaped like a roller coaster. The point of this book is not to impose preconceived concepts upon you but to enable you to do your own thing with confidence and to enjoy the delightful and well balanced harmony which you have created.

A point on **medicinal herbs** is important to make. Herbs can be powerful healing tools, but may also harm the user. Never try any herbal formula without consulting a qualified medical herbalist first. When trying out culinary herbs, try just a little at first in case you have any allergic reactions. If in doubt, don't!

2.	*Planning your herb garden*

First decide what **kind** of herb garden you want. This seems the easy bit, but there are so many different kinds of herb garden that it is easy to let your imagination run away with you and turn your whole site into one gigantic herb garden. Some people settle for a basic twenty culinary herbs but others become totally addicted and have collections of many hundreds of different plants. Apart from culinary herbs, there are medicinal herbs, dyeing and textile herbs, butterfly food plants, nectar plants for specialist honeys and herbs for brewing. **Theme gardens** provide interesting talking points: Medieval and Bible gardens are popular as are Renaissance and Shakespeare gardens. You can even develop a Witch Herb Garden or a Roman Herb Plot!

To some extent you will be constrained by the **site** itself. It is no good for instance trying to establish a Mediterranean garden in a Welsh peat bog. In these circumstances you can either try and modify the site or work on the basis of *if you can't beat 'em, join 'em*, and we will come on to that later in the chapter.

But back to the beginning; we will work on the supposition that you want a garden that will supply most of the herbs you need for the kitchen, that will look attractive and perfume the air around where you want to laze in the summer sun.

The really good news about herbs is that you don't have to keep composting, mulching and fertilising them. In fact many positively resent such fussing; it leads to rank, stringy growth which ruins their flavour and lessens their resistance to winter weather. Nevertheless herbs do hate compressed, wet inorganic growing conditions, which are the sort almost invariably left behind when the builders have finished. So if you have just taken over the sort of new garden which consists of broken bricks, odd shaped bits of metal and puddle-strewn areas of sand, you can either laboriously extract the rubbish by hand and then dig in peat or rotted dung or else take the easy way out.

This is to cover the whole mess in gravel to ensure good drainage (perhaps with land drain pipes) and then put at least 50cm of good top soil on top of that. This applies not just to herbs but to any garden. It is interesting to note that the medieval designers of monastic herb  gardens also grew their herbs in raised beds to avoid compressed soil and water logged roots.

Ideally your **soil** should be brown and crumbly, to give your herbs air spaces around the roots. The problem with *clay* soils is that the particles are so fine that they clog together in a solid mass. Dig in processed seaweed and other soil conditioners to help. *Sandy* soils are slightly less of a problem, but because they are free draining, many of the plant nutrients will get washed out. Some herbs need more feeding than others. *Tarragon* and *thyme* for instance can cope with impoverished soil much more successfully than *horseradish* and *dill*.

Then there is the problem of **acidity and alkalinity.** If in doubt go for the alkaline side as most of the best tasting herbs prefer it. Check the other gardens in your area. If they have *Rhododendrons* and *azaleas* the soil is acid and so to grow herbs like *lavenders* and *thymes* successfully, you will have to dig some lime into the garden. This is a lot easier than the reverse problem, that of trying to turn alkaline soil (eg chalk downland) acid. However if you don't have acid soil and you want to grow *star anise* and many of the North American herbs, then raised beds or patio pots, containing ericaceous compost, are probably your best solution.

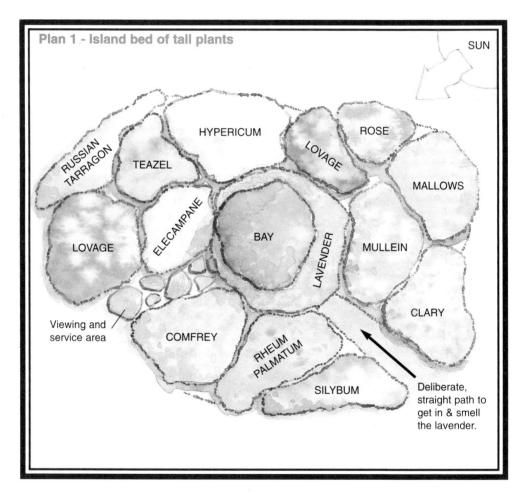

Plan 1 - Island bed of tall plants

SUN

HYPERICUM
ROSE
RUSSIAN TARRAGON
TEAZEL
LOVAGE
MALLOWS
ELECAMPANE
BAY
LAVENDER
MULLEIN
LOVAGE
CLARY
Viewing and service area
COMFREY
RHEUM PALMATUM
SILYBUM
Deliberate, straight path to get in & smell the lavender.

If you have taken over an **established garden,** someone else has already done the initial work for you and it is just a matter of taking out the weeds and plants you don't want (pot them up and sell them or give them away) digging it over and planting your herbs. Of course, you could clear the site completely, redesign it, alter the levels, put in terraces, pergolas, water features and patios. It will look great but the wonderful moment when you sprinkle delicious home grown chives over your potato salad for the first time will be much further off.

However you prepare your herb garden, remember that most herbs need a lot of **sunlight** so if the garden-to-be is over-hung by trees and shrubs, they must be cut back before you plant.

Where to site your herb garden

People often think that herb gardens should be put by the back door so that you can go and pick a handful for cooking purposes without having to walk too far. This is an unfortunate idea on several counts. The garden is supposed to be a pleasure and

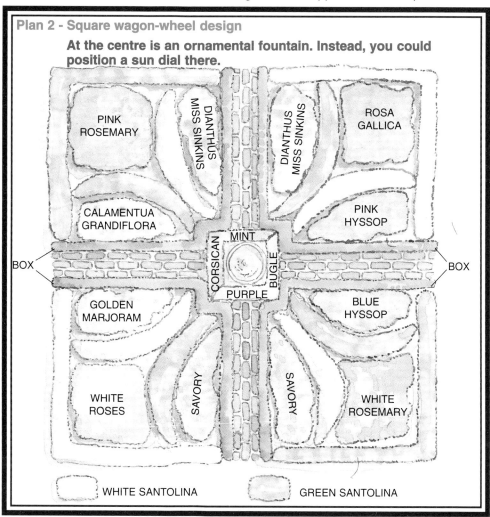

Plan 2 - Square wagon-wheel design

At the centre is an ornamental fountain. Instead, you could position a sun dial there.

PINK ROSEMARY

DIANTHUS MISS SINKINS

DIANTHUS MISS SINKINS

ROSA GALLICA

CALAMENTUA GRANDIFLORA

PINK HYSSOP

BOX

CORSICAN MINT

BUGLE

PURPLE

BOX

GOLDEN MARJORAM

BLUE HYSSOP

WHITE ROSES

SAVORY

SAVORY

WHITE ROSEMARY

WHITE SANTOLINA   GREEN SANTOLINA

there is not much point in embarking on a garden in the first place if it is too much of a drag to walk through it to pick a sprig of mint; better to live in a flat instead. Most house-cooks today, particularly the executive sort who are always in a hurry, have their meals planned to the final second so that last minute crises don't occur. Modern gardens are usually so small anyway!

5

Bay

A *bay tree* is probably the most expensive purchase for your herb garden. One will provide enough leaves for your needs growing to 3.5m over 20 years. Has small yellow flowers turning (sometimes) to purple berries. Site carefully in rich soil, well drained but never drying out, sheltered from cold winds (especially from the North and East). Does well in a large pot on a sunny patio, but feed well. *Bays* can be clipped in to pyramids and their trunks trained into serpentines. The leaves provide a robust flavour and go well in game dishes. If given a *bay*, check it's not a *laurel* with which they are often confused - the leaves smell quite different!

2. Bay
(Laurus nobilis)

Having dismissed the human aspect, look at it from the plant's point of view. Back doors are normally on the north side of the house - the side that gets least light, and thus provides the worst possible growing conditions. Even less desirable is the fact that around the back door is a **sacrifice area,** into which cats, dogs and children are cast out to perform activities wholly at odds with the purpose of a herb garden.

Instead site your garden at the front or side of the house in full sun. The cover illustration shows just how attractive this can be. Few things can provide so warm a welcome to your home or conjure up such an appetite than an approach through aromatic herbs. They are particularly delightful when combined with climbing and bush *roses* or with *honeysuckle*. The effect of the climbers is to soften the right angle between the wall of the house and the ground which, if only low growing herbs were planted, would otherwise be unpleasantly harsh. It is true that most herbs look utterly bedraggled in winter, but interplanting with autumn and spring *bulbs* will shorten the empty season considerably. Winter flowering *pansies* are also appropriate with the additional virtue that their flowers are edible and can be used to brighten winter salads.

Formal and informal herb gardens

Formal herb gardens have lots of geometrical lines and look as though they have been carefully designed to need a lot of hard work. Don't let this fool you, the best informal gardens have been even more carefully designed than the formal ones but the clever thing is that it doesn't show. Moreover the appearance of needing less maintenance is an illusion as it is much easier to weed along straight lines particularly with machinery than it is a free flowing shape. In both cases, it is fundamental to the design to allow yourself access to the plants.

This particularly applies to herb gardens because you are not only going to maintain your plants but harvest them as well. Many people plant up a **wagon wheel design** and then wonder where they are going to put their feet when they come to weed it.

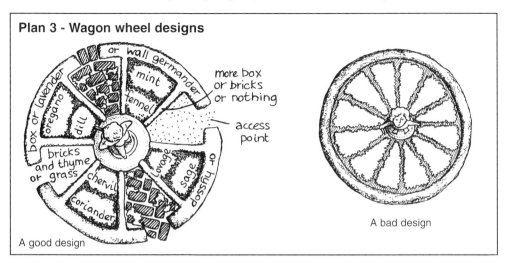

Plan 3 - Wagon wheel designs

or wall germander
mint
fennel
more box
or bricks
or nothing
box or lavender
oregano
dill
access point
bricks and thyme or grass
chervil
coriander
lovage
sage
hyssop to
A good design

A bad design

The **bad design** is a recipe for disaster. It is over crowded, the angles are too tight, there is no way of reaching the centre without trampling the plants and it still only contains twelve varieties.

The **good design** has only half the segments planted up but with two different herbs in each. Alternate segments can be walked on to get to the herbs. It will need some of its grass cut by hand, since the mower won't get to the middle. You might put another circle in the centre, with a *bay* tree, statue or fountain. This does, however, increase the size of the design and also the cost.

If you have room only for a small design, try a **chequer board** instead. It is really the same thing as a wagon wheel with straight lines replacing the curved lines.

A Chequer board herb garden

As Medieval developed into Renaissance, **parterres** became popular. These were very formal designs in which, as the name suggests, plants were alternated with paths of differing textures that could be walked on. These were *pleasure gardens* and materials tried out for the pathways included sea shells, coal dust and ground up brick all of which make an interesting foil to the greenness of the adjacent leaves. A modern example of this can be seen in the newly laid out garden at Tredegar House in Gwent (near exit 28 of the M4). Although this is a very large project, it is worth visiting to get ideas to try out at home.

Herb garden walls

Most of the original herb gardens were laid out in monasteries and castle grounds and thus had **walls** around them, The walls not only kept out enemies and predatory animals but also gave a sense of spiritual unity in the garden. Within this boundary the herb gardens themselves had hedges and edges, sometimes several. Originally these may have been to stop dirt getting on culinary herbs. More importantly however, they provide a micro-climate which is so good for Mediterranean herbs that dislike the cold wet winds of an English winter.

Today walls are still often used in a herb garden design but they are a mixed blessing. They are **good** in that they will provide a windbreak on the lee side stretching horizontally to about three to six times the height of the wall. Plants grown against a South facing wall will bask in the warmth reflected from the bricks and mature faster.

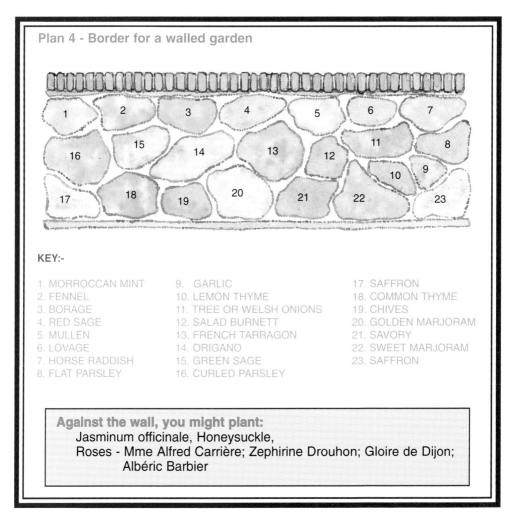

Plan 4 - Border for a walled garden

KEY:-

1. MORROCCAN MINT
2. FENNEL
3. BORAGE
4. RED SAGE
5. MULLEN
6. LOVAGE
7. HORSE RADDISH
8. FLAT PARSLEY

9. GARLIC
10. LEMON THYME
11. TREE OR WELSH ONIONS
12. SALAD BURNETT
13. FRENCH TARRAGON
14. ORIGANO
15. GREEN SAGE
16. CURLED PARSLEY

17. SAFFRON
18. COMMON THYME
19. CHIVES
20. GOLDEN MARJORAM
21. SAVORY
22. SWEET MARJORAM
23. SAFFRON

Against the wall, you might plant:
Jasminum officinale, Honeysuckle,
Roses - Mme Alfred Carrière; Zephirine Drouhon; Gloire de Dijon;
Albéric Barbier

The **bad** news is that some plants such as *rosemary* and *hyssop* actually prefer to have an air current passing over them and should therefore never be planted against a wall unless it is south facing (to catch currents of warm air off the bricks).

Walls also block out a lot of light and keep nearby plants rather dry, so give extra **water** as needed. Walls erected across slopes will create frost pockets as air **frost** behaves very much like water and flows down hill. Any obstruction acts like a dam, so herbs should never be planted on the uphill side of a wall, unless ***weep holes*** have been left in the brickwork to allow the frosty air through. If you already have a wall and it belongs to your house or your garage, it would probably cause family upset to knock holes in it and you will have to plant elsewhere. The alternative to a wall on a slope is a hedge: not only does it let the cold air flow through but it is cheaper. The opposite applies if you are able to plant against a wall on the down side of a slope, in which case the wall will prevent the frost flowing around the stems of your plants.

Walls can have **plants** growing in, up and on top of them. Such plantings soften hard lines and give an impression of maturity. To help establish growth along the top of a wall, the stonework should be irregular. Old stone walls are easy and cavity blocks easier still, though these will look hideous until they have aged. Possibly the most difficult are new brick walls.

Try **sowing** seeds in a little compost on the wall top, or grow suitable plants in biodegradable pots wedged into the gaps with loose stones which can be removed later.

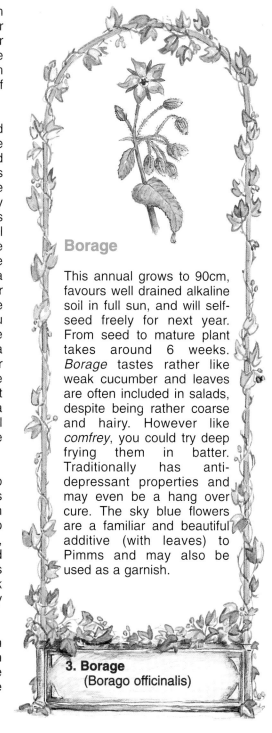

Borage

This annual grows to 90cm, favours well drained alkaline soil in full sun, and will self-seed freely for next year. From seed to mature plant takes around 6 weeks. *Borage* tastes rather like weak cucumber and leaves are often included in salads, despite being rather coarse and hairy. However like *comfrey*, you could try deep frying them in batter. Traditionally has anti-depressant properties and may even be a hang over cure. The sky blue flowers are a familiar and beautiful additive (with leaves) to Pimms and may also be used as a garnish.

*3. Borage
(Borago officinalis)*

The swiss roll

The odd brick or stone can be left out of the wall whilst it is being built and replaced by a piece of rotted, rolled up turf, with the original roots on the outside and the edge of the **swiss roll** facing outwards impregnated with herb seed.

Another idea is to cut plastic drain pipes to the size of the hole, fill them with compost and treat them as normal pots until the plants are growing strongly, then stick them sideways in to the holes in the wall. In this way, the tubes can be slid out and the plants easily be replaced from one season the the next, but be sure to water them regularly and well.

Hanging baskets can also be hung on the wall either from brackets secured to the masonry by rawlplugs or from brackets slung over the top of the wall. Small **aromatic plants** are best appreciated at waist, or better, nose height. Raised sinks, old fonts and window boxes have all been used, or you can design your own support!

A hanging basket

Spreading layers of carpet

Spreading layers of carpet on the ground for six months is well known as an organic way of killing the weeds underneath. The bad news is that you still have to think of a *green* method of disposing the bits of carpet when you have finished with them. Old motor tyres can be used as cheap pots, pond edgings and as weights on mulches, but because they contain metal, they present even greater problems when their time is up.

<table>
<tr><td>**3.**</td><td>*Buying and caring for your plants*</td></tr>
</table>

There are only two ways of stocking your herb garden: from seed or by obtaining already growing plants. If a friend offers you cuttings, because *they're easy* ask her to grow them on for you. There is no point in making difficulties for yourself at the beginning.

Plants can be purchased from garden centres, specialist nurseries, by mail order or begging from friends. Each method has its traps and advantages and it is up to you which you choose. **Garden centres** are relatively cheap. Most have a reasonable selection of herbs and all their pots should be in immaculate condition. You can select not just the variety of herb you want, but the actual plant itself. The disadvantage for

spring purchases is that the plants will have come from the pristine conditions of a specialist herb raiser, who may have been badgered by the garden centre to let them have the plants as early as possible in the season. These plants will have been forced and had little opportunity to build up any resistance to disease. Taken out of their cosy green house, stripped of the carefully formulated compost in which they were nurtured and set out in the cold wet earth of the purchaser's garden, surrounded by bugs and blasted by the frosts, winds and rain of an English spring, they are unlikely to last twenty four hours!

Garden centres depend upon a quick turnaround of stock and often, particularly early in the season, the plants may be very soft and immature. So keep your little plant on the kitchen window sill at least for as long as it takes the roots to show through the bottom of the pot. This will tell you that a viable rootball has developed. Then when you plant it out on the next fine day, you can be sure that some of the original compost will come with it, which will give it a much better start. Another problem with garden centres is that the quality of **advice** is not always as good as it could be. Some assistants are extremely knowledgeable and helpful, but you might just get an untrained teenage girl straight from Santa's grotto to sell you your spring plants. Of course, garden centres are also in the business of selling **books** and they would obviously like you to buy one of them!

Four Thieves Vinegar.

This recipe, dating from the 1722 plague outbreak in Marseilles, is said to have allowed the four thieves from whom it took its name to rob the sick and dying with impunity. Gather the tops of *wormwood, mint, rosemary, sage, rue, lavender* and infuse them for two weeks on a sunny windowsill in red wine vinegar with a generous amount of *garlic* and pinches of *nutmeg, cloves* and *cinnamon*. Add *Camphor* before liberally splashing over one's clothes and body. Modern research has proven all the herbs used have antiseptic properties.

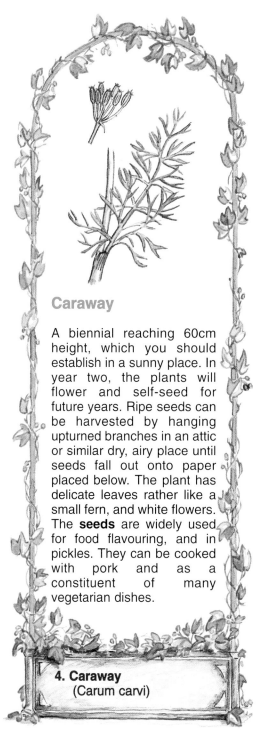

Caraway

A biennial reaching 60cm height, which you should establish in a sunny place. In year two, the plants will flower and self-seed for future years. Ripe seeds can be harvested by hanging upturned branches in an attic or similar dry, airy place until seeds fall out onto paper placed below. The plant has delicate leaves rather like a small fern, and white flowers. The **seeds** are widely used for food flavouring, and in pickles. They can be cooked with pork and as a constituent of many vegetarian dishes.

4. Caraway
(Carum carvi)

These days, there is almost certain to be a **specialist herb nursery** close to where you live. Ask for details from the *British Herb Trade Association* (see **Appendix**). Most reputable herb farms belong to the BHTA and offer expert advice, good service and excellent plants. Several have magnificent display gardens where you can see what your garden will look like when it matures. Others have no interest whatever in gardens but only in plants. These are often the most interesting because while they look an absolute tip, this is because all their resources are tied up in producing a really unusual range of plants, many of which may be unique to that one nursery alone.

Unlike garden centres, which only sell the final product, the nurseries produce their own plants and death and disaster rear their heads every day so don't be surprised to see the odd casualties about the place. Nevertheless don't buy anything less than perfect (unless it is at reduced price!). A favourite bit of media advice is not to buy anything that is *pot bound*. "Turn the pot over," they say, "and check it." My advice is **don't**. There can be no quicker route to being thrown out of a nursery or garden centre by an irate manager than mistreating his plants.

But does **pot bound** matter anyway? Like many well-meaning generalisations, the answer is **yes, but.**

To keep flies away from your barbecue, burn *santolina* and *wormwood* on the fire.

It certainly applies in the case of single stemmed items like trees, *lavenders*, *rosemary* and some *sages*, where the roots will be seen to circle the pot trying to escape in their desperate search for nutrients. Such a plant may contain more dying root than compost and will be retarded so that even if rescue comes in time to avert death, recovery will be slow. On the other hand, some creeping plants which throw up lots of new shoots can be a good buy if you split the roots with a fresh shoot on each one. *Solomon's seal, mints* and some *thymes* particularly lend themselves to this treatment. *Lemon grass* forms dense clumps in large pots and these can be split with an axe. This is a quick and reliable way to bulk up your garden - a great morale booster to the beginner. The advice then is to **buy it and try it**, but always look for lots of shoots coming out of the pot.

Another way of buying established plants is to write to a nursery specialising in **mail order** supplies. Of course, you won't know exactly what you are buying, and whether the plants received will have stood up to the journey. Try to find a friend who has used the firm, and take advice on the service and the quality of the supplies. A good nursery should refund or replace plants which arrive damaged, and also offer good telephone advice. Once you have found a reliable one, stick to it.

Not all growers **pack** their plants the same way. Some nurseries despatch their plants bare rooted, wrapped in sphagnum moss, and others prefer to

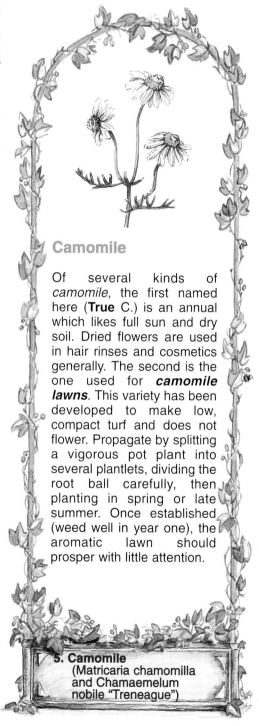

Camomile

Of several kinds of *camomile*, the first named here (**True** C.) is an annual which likes full sun and dry soil. Dried flowers are used in hair rinses and cosmetics generally. The second is the one used for *camomile lawns*. This variety has been developed to make low, compact turf and does not flower. Propagate by splitting a vigorous pot plant into several plantlets, dividing the root ball carefully, then planting in spring or late summer. Once established (weed well in year one), the aromatic lawn should prosper with little attention.

5. Camomile
(Matricaria chamomilla and Chamaemelum nobile "Treneague")

Maibowle
This is traditionally drunk on May day in Germany. It is prepared by steeping sprigs of *woodruff* in Rhenish wine. Ex-pats in California enhanced the old recipe by substituting brandy for the wine and adding crushed *raspberries*.

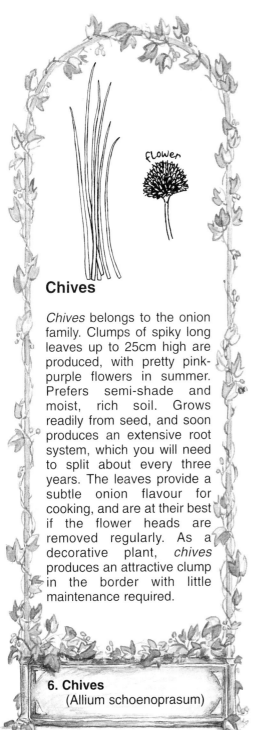

Flower

Chives

Chives belongs to the onion family. Clumps of spiky long leaves up to 25cm high are produced, with pretty pink-purple flowers in summer. Prefers semi-shade and moist, rich soil. Grows readily from seed, and soon produces an extensive root system, which you will need to split about every three years. The leaves provide a subtle onion flavour for cooking, and are at their best if the flower heads are removed regularly. As a decorative plant, *chives* produces an attractive clump in the border with little maintenance required.

6. Chives
(Allium schoenoprasum)

send out plants straight from the pot with their compost undisturbed in the belief that this gives more reliable establishment in their new home. **Speed** is essential and so the best growers either use a Royal Mail premium service or a reliable courier. This is not cheap but it does ensure the customer gets healthy plants. If you choose to buy like this, it is worth ordering a lot

of plants at once, as the cost of carriage should be proportionately less.

No reputable herb nursery will sell you annuals like *basil* and *dill* by mail order. They rarely survive so it is always cheaper to buy seed. If you order out of season, most growers will leave despatch until the spring. You then have the certainty that if the plants die during the winter, they will be the grower's loss and not yours. Moreover, having paid for the plants, you will be at the head of the queue should they be in short supply.

When your plants arrive, check the parcel. If damaged, don't sign the slip saying that it has been received in good condition. If the plants inside are dehydrated or slimy, notify the grower immediately. Otherwise unpack them carefully, making sure you keep the labels with the appropriate plants. **Small plants** are very fragile and many will have been bent into odd shapes during transit. Pot them up into good compost and, if dry, stand them in a saucer of water for half an hour. The reasons for not planting them out immediately are that they will appreciate a bit of spoiling after their journey and more importantly, that at least some of the outside leaves may have rotted. This will make the plants specially attractive to slugs until they are growing strongly again. The extra attention you give them initially will be repaid many times over in the months to come.

4.	*Seeds and seedlings*

Propagation sounds complicated; it isn't. It is simply the process of getting lots of new plants from one parent plant. If plants hadn't been able to do it themselves for millions of years they would have gone extinct. Nevertheless, many herbs find the conditions in a British garden unfamiliar and will respond to a helping hand. *Rosemary* for instance is one of many of our common herbs whose real home is beside the Mediterranean. It grows happily in most of England and Western Scotland, but rarely reproduces itself here, though it grows easily from cuttings or seeds sown in warm conditions.

Collecting seed from your own plants is quite easy! Pick ripe seed heads on a dry day when they have gone hard (and perhaps papery) - there should be no trace of green left. Place heads on a paper-covered tray, keep dry, then shake on to paper when they split over the following days. Keep fully dry seeds in a labelled sealed plastic bag in a cool, dry, dark place.

Seeds hold a range of terrors for beginners. Fortunately it only takes a little advice and experience to make most of these spooks disappear. Growing from seed is relatively inexpensive and can give an enormous amount of satisfaction. For many people, turning a packet of something resembling dust into scented, flowering plants is the ultimate in creativity.

The two most frequently heard cries are, "I planted them and nothing happened" or "I planted them, they came up beautifully then the whole lot fell over and died." Such heartbreak is preventable by following simple procedures, so much so that by the end of the season you will be trying to find a lucky recipient for your surplus.

The first rule is to use fresh seed. Some seeds have to be sown absolutely fresh to get perfect results; amongst these are *angelica* and *pasque flower*. Parsley is particularly infamous in this respect: most people fail completely unless they are using absolutely fresh seed. Other seeds lie around in the ground doing nothing for about eighteen months whilst the novice gardener's frustration increases and enthusiasm wanes.

You will know the age of seed you beg from a friend's garden or buy direct from a seed supplier. If buying from a shop, check the date of production on the packet - don't buy anything that isn't date stamped.

Flowers can brighten up any salad.
Try *roses, violas, pelargoniums, marigolds, rocket, mallow, chives, bergamot, alliums* and *rosemarys*. If you run out of *borage* flowers to decorate your Pimms any of these will do instead. In the Middle Ages, *pinks* were usually floated in gone-off claret to disguise the rancid taste.

Choose your **annuals** - all seed catalogues and most packets say which these are. They should always be sown in the spring as the grown-up plants won't survive winter but fortunately they are usually very cheap. The group includes some of the most tasty herbs such as *coriander, salad rocket* and *basil.*

Perennials are those plants whose seeds naturally drop down to the ground when they ripen in autumn and spend the winter buried close to the surface, before sprouting in the spring. Many of these, *sweet cicely* and *cowslips* for example, bear seeds which refuse to germinate until they have been exposed to **frost**. So, keep the seed packets *in the fridge* for three weeks during the winter, before sowing them in a seed tray on a warm windowsill. Perennials can be **started** in the autumn, but once this is done, they have to be kept going in ideal conditions which you need to provide for them. This is obviously an inconvenience!

To obtain **successful germination** seeds need warmth, light and air. These are surprisingly difficult to provide in a garden and so sowing indoors, in a greenhouse or

Sowing your seeds

1. Ensure your trays and pots have good drainage holes.

2. Almost fill pots and trays with sterile compost and water sparingly.

3. Sprinkle a few seeds in each pot or tray; press down lightly on larger seeds.

even in a home made garden frame is recommended. Wet particles of fine soil can pack around a seed literally suffocating it. If the particles are dry, there will be none of the moisture that your seedling needs to grow. If they are hot and wet, the seed will become fungal and rot. This sounds very off-putting but it need not be. Just buy seed trays and some seed compost from your garden centre and follow the instructions on the compost packet. The compost will have been specially formulated to provide air spaces around the seedlings' developing roots. Unless the seeds are very large, it is unnecessary to bury them, in fact some like *winter savory* will fail completely if they are not exposed to light.

Provide just enough **moisture** to keep the compost slightly and evenly damp, never wet. If you cover the tray, leave sufficient space between the surface of the compost and the cover to allow air to enter freely. This prevents condensation and the build up of fungi spores that get everywhere. Seeds appear to appreciate one anothers' company and two sown together do better than one on its own. However, too many in close proximity catch one anothers' diseases and drop dead, so always sow sparingly and evenly.

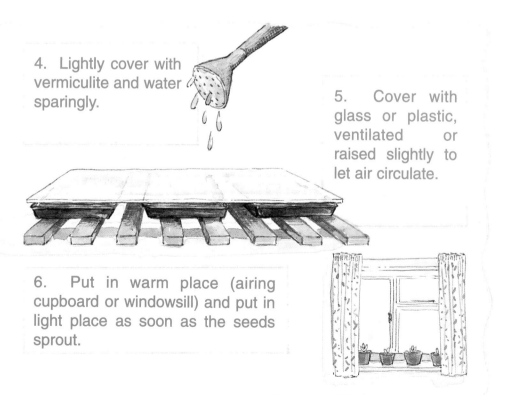

4. Lightly cover with vermiculite and water sparingly.

5. Cover with glass or plastic, ventilated or raised slightly to let air circulate.

6. Put in warm place (airing cupboard or windowsill) and put in light place as soon as the seeds sprout.

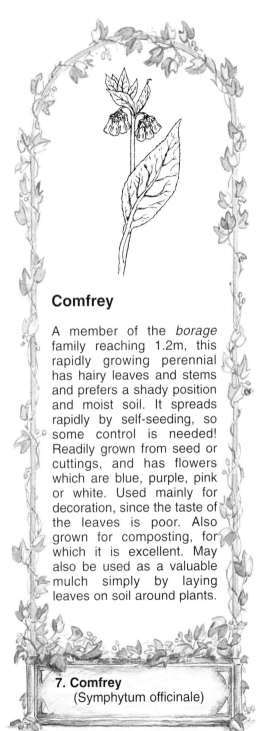

Comfrey

A member of the *borage* family reaching 1.2m, this rapidly growing perennial has hairy leaves and stems and prefers a shady position and moist soil. It spreads rapidly by self-seeding, so some control is needed! Readily grown from seed or cuttings, and has flowers which are blue, purple, pink or white. Used mainly for decoration, since the taste of the leaves is poor. Also grown for composting, for which it is excellent. May also be used as a valuable mulch simply by laying leaves on soil around plants.

7. Comfrey
(Symphytum officinale)

It is now possible to purchase **sowing modules** which consist of small cells large enough for one or two seeds. The advantage of these is that once germinated, the seedling can be removed easily without disturbing the roots. Although suitable for almost all seeds, these are really useful for starting annuals indoors, rather than risk wasting seed by sowing directly into outdoor soil. The modules usually come with a blunt-spiked tool resembling a mini tank trap. This is to expel the seedlings from the module when they are ready; it is *not* for ramming the compost down in to the cells. Normal pressure with the palm of the hand should be sufficient for this and the surplus compost can be lightly brushed off and used for the next module. Even though there are holes in the bottom of the cells, the compost will stay in them when you move them unless they have been excessively watered.

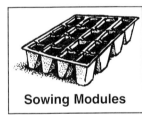

Sowing Modules

If you have plenty of seed you can sow **direct** into your garden, but this is fraught with hazards. Wood lice and slugs may annihilate your seedlings before you even realise that they have germinated. This is one reason why nothing seems to have happened after the seeds have been sown. Then the soil may be too dry, too wet or too cold, condemning the seeds to failure. If they do come up, how do you recognise your babies from the pack of nature's thugs which are always lying in wait for delicate newcomers? To a beginner all seeds look the same and yours may well have been choked to death before you realise which of the small green things should have been pulled out!

What to do with your seedlings

Once your seeds have sprouted (vigorously of course) they will set about growing roots, and will soon have exhausted the space available to them. Now comes the next step.

With **modules**, you will find that by gently lifting the plant, the whole thing will come away from the tray with the roots and compost exactly replicating the shape of the module, much as you once made sand castles. With **seed trays**, things are slightly different. You will have heard the expression *pricking out* used by gardening enthusiasts. Actually this is an utter waste of time and the plants don`t like it much either. Seedlings in a well sown tray will have formed a dense root mat below the surface and the easiest way to deal with them is to take a large slice of this pancake-like mat and break off bits containing several plants. In this way you won't stress every single plant in the tray. In a couple of weeks time, if the divided clumps still seem over crowded, you can snip off the surplus and eat them immediately.

Now that you have a lot of little plants in clumps or modules lying on the kitchen table you have to decide whether to *plant them out* or *pot them on*.

Planting out the seedlings

The ideal is to plant them out in a green house, but if this luxury is not available, you can plant them outside. There are ways you can increase their chances of survival in their new world. Carefully **weed** the patch they are to go in, and make sure this new bed is **warm.**

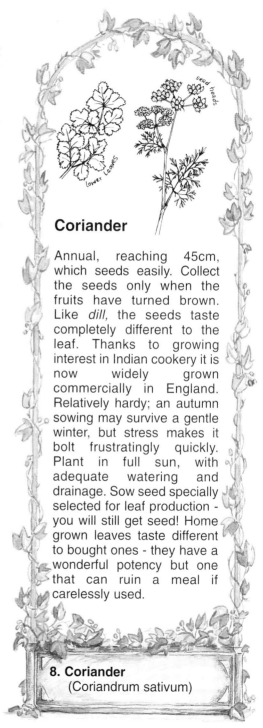

Coriander

Annual, reaching 45cm, which seeds easily. Collect the seeds only when the fruits have turned brown. Like *dill,* the seeds taste completely different to the leaf. Thanks to growing interest in Indian cookery it is now widely grown commercially in England. Relatively hardy; an autumn sowing may survive a gentle winter, but stress makes it bolt frustratingly quickly. Plant in full sun, with adequate watering and drainage. Sow seed specially selected for leaf production - you will still get seed! Home grown leaves taste different to bought ones - they have a wonderful potency but one that can ruin a meal if carelessly used.

8. Coriander
(Coriandrum sativum)

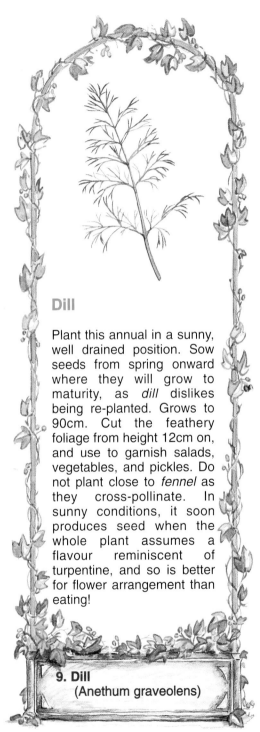

Dill

Plant this annual in a sunny, well drained position. Sow seeds from spring onward where they will grow to maturity, as *dill* dislikes being re-planted. Grows to 90cm. Cut the feathery foliage from height 12cm on, and use to garnish salads, vegetables, and pickles. Do not plant close to *fennel* as they cross-pollinate. In sunny conditions, it soon produces seed when the whole plant assumes a flavour reminiscent of turpentine, and so is better for flower arrangement than eating!

9. Dill
(Anethum graveolens)

You can do both things by putting down a layer of **black plastic sheeting** over the new bed six weeks before you plant out. The plastic absorbs the sun's rays and at the same time suffocates the emerging weeds. A black permeable membrane is best because it lets water through, but it costs more. Peg the sheeting down or cover the edges with soil and stones. Pellets or beer traps should be laid for **slugs** a couple of days before planting out.

When **planting out**, keep as much as possible of the root ball and attached compost in one piece. Place in a scooped-out hole with the surface of the compost level with the soil surface. Fill in the gaps with soil and lightly firm round with your fingers, adding extra soil if necessary. Water straight away, and keep watering on the following days whenever the plant needs it. Avoid planting on very sunny or windy days as these will cause the seedlings to dry out. If you still feel your babies need further nurturing, a **fleece** or **cloche** from your garden centre will provide extra protection, especially when frost is forecast. The problem with cloches is that they are difficult to water and irritating to pick under. At least with a fleece, the water drips through, but they are inclined to blow away unless well weighted down.

If you have made a **mulch** out of lawn clippings, this will not be much use for your seedling herbs. Most varieties, particularly Mediterranean ones, can't stand anything cold and clammy near their roots. A mulch of fine gravel is much more acceptable and helps keep in moisture as well as deter weed growth. Your lawn mulch can be kept until the end of the season and then dug in around where you are going to plant *chives, lovage* and *parsley* the following year.

These greedy feeders will appreciate the extra nutrients. Herbs though, for the most part, have a much better flavour if they are kept away from **fertilisers.** That said, if you are sowing straight into the garden, *dill* and *chervil* have a much better colour if a little straight **nitrogen fertiliser** is applied to the ground immediately prior to putting the seeds or plants in.

Potting on the seedlings

Take your seedlings - in little clumps or modules - and plant in a larger pot with potting compost, either to grow them on before planting outside, or to keep them indoors or on a greenhouse bench. Make sure the pot is large enough to avoid the need to re-pot later. Do not over-firm the compost, and be sure to water well.

Add a thin layer of vermiculite on the surface

Keeping your herbs in a pot on the window sill or patio is easy to begin with, but gets more difficult later. Indoors you can see when they are wilting due to lack of water and light and they won't suffer from bug attacks, but they will soon use up their limited supply of nutrients, so you must **feed** them regularly. This may cause a slight loss of flavour; liquid or powder feed added to the water is easiest.

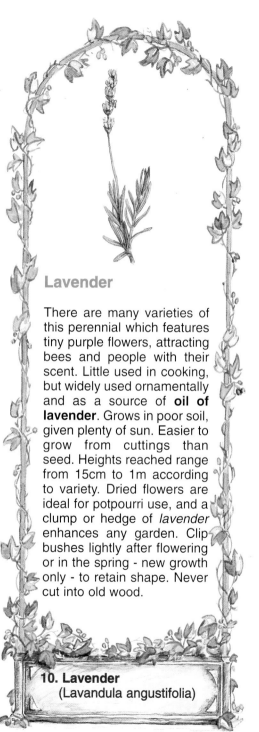

Lavender

There are many varieties of this perennial which features tiny purple flowers, attracting bees and people with their scent. Little used in cooking, but widely used ornamentally and as a source of **oil of lavender**. Grows in poor soil, given plenty of sun. Easier to grow from cuttings than seed. Heights reached range from 15cm to 1m according to variety. Dried flowers are ideal for potpourri use, and a clump or hedge of *lavender* enhances any garden. Clip bushes lightly after flowering or in the spring - new growth only - to retain shape. Never cut into old wood.

10. Lavender
(Lavandula angustifolia)

The two difficulties indoors are light and warmth. There is never as much **light** as there seems inside a house (as camera users will know). If the light is too poor, find another site for your plants. Unless the plants are up against double glazing, window sills are **cold** places; a single pane of glass is a poor insulator. Curtains cut the pots off from the warmth of the radiator so always bring your plants inside the curtains at night. Plants in pots on a patio are far more susceptible to **frost** damage than those planted in the ground because their roots are deprived of the protection of the soil. For this reason, use as large a pot as possible and try to bring the pot into a conservatory in winter.

Annuals in pots are easy: just grow them, eat them and start again. As for perennials, take a first cut and then they should be strong enough to be planted outside and to look after themselves. Whatever you do with your plants, they are going to need water, but those in the ground are going to need far less fussing over than those in pots. Many herbs hate getting their leaves wet and the easiest way of dealing with those is to put a seep hose along the ground. If they are in pots, they can be left in the sink for twenty minutes, but don't forget to rescue them or they will become water logged and the roots will rot.

Collecting seed

One of your first plants to set **seed** will be *coriander*. This perplexes people who are growing it for its leaves. "Why has it done that?" they ask. Though it is thought to be related to drought stress, excess day length and too much phosphate, the real answer is that no one knows for sure. Soon the rest of your herbs will flower and set seed. You can either collect these on a dry summer day and use them as flavourings during the winter or keep them in a cool, dark place for sowing next spring. The advantage of collecting your seeds is that eventually you will build up a strain of herbs that does best in your own garden. All the less well adapted plants will have died off before setting seed. Also a seed packet may just contain more than one variety of the species named on the packet. If your seeds have grown up as a mix of varieties, you can select seeds only from the ones you like best for planting next year.

Roasting garlic alongside the potatoes

with the Sunday joint is an old English tradition. Try it and you will find the *garlic* has virtually no smell at all.

Pruning perennial herbs

If you don't eat your herbs, many perennials will become straggly and unattractive - for example *rosemary, lavender, hyssop,* also some *sages* and *thymes.* The **best time** to prune them is immediately before or after flowering when they are at their most vigorous. Contrary to what you will be told, they should never be cut back in the autumn or winter. The rule with *lavender* and *rosemary* is never to cut into the previous year's wood though it is worth a gamble with badly neglected plants. Sometimes they show remarkable powers in coming back from the dead, but never rely on this. It is always your most precious plant that won't survive the treatment.

Pruning back top shoots

Cut off the old flower stalks, and the top growth to make a neat slightly rounded profile once flowering is over. Remove shoots which intrude into another plant's patch. Then in spring, cut off any dead wood lost during the winter.

Gotu Kola.

This is reputed to have as many uses as scientists have given it names. Amongst these are Hydrocotyle asiatica, Acenna asiatica and Centella asiatica. It has recently become popular as a cure for arthritis; previously it was reputed to be a sure fire cure for leprosy and, in Chinese tradition, it is supposed to enable you to live long past your 120th birthday. Many Americans regard it as poisonous.

Bay trees deserve special mention as shaped ones are so expensive that it is worth designing your own as a centre piece to your garden. If you use a lot of *bay* in the kitchen, you can clip your tree into shape as you eat it. This seems more sensible than trying to do the whole tree at once and throwing away the clippings. Even if you hate the flavour, a severely clipped *bay* will always look better than one which has been allowed to grow straggly.

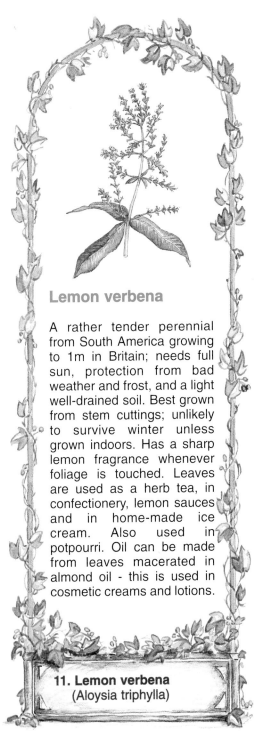

Lemon verbena

A rather tender perennial from South America growing to 1m in Britain; needs full sun, protection from bad weather and frost, and a light well-drained soil. Best grown from stem cuttings; unlikely to survive winter unless grown indoors. Has a sharp lemon fragrance whenever foliage is touched. Leaves are used as a herb tea, in confectionery, lemon sauces and in home-made ice cream. Also used in potpourri. Oil can be made from leaves macerated in almond oil - this is used in cosmetic creams and lotions.

11. Lemon verbena
(Aloysia triphylla)

Shaped bay trees

Give your clipped tree some fertiliser to make up for what you have taken away from it. It is important to keep it growing strongly in order to resist the diseases to which bays are susceptible. **Bay weevil** and **scale insects** are two particular pests which can be countered by spraying with Malathion during the first hot week in spring. If you are going to use the leaves in the kitchen, read the spray label carefully - note the recommended interval between application and harvest and stick to it.

Taking soft wood cuttings

Like water divining, the ability to take **cuttings** is a gift from God. Whether you have it or not can be found only by trying it. Have a go - otherwise you will deprive yourself of an enormous amount of pleasure, and perhaps profit, in the years to come. Anyway, by the end of your first year, the plants you bought from the garden centre during the spring will now be so big and luxuriant that the temptation to try a few cuttings will be almost irresistible.

There are two basic types of cuttings - **soft wood** and **hard wood**. Soft wood cuttings are taken from the current year's growth and are faster than those taken from the hard wood of previous years. **Soft wood cuttings** can be taken from woody perennials like *rosemary, thyme, lavender, sage* and *bay trees*. This also is a useful way to prune your plants.

Choose a length of soft wood, which you can recognise because it is soft and green, unlike the old wood on the same stem which is usually rigid and brown. Snip diagonally across the bottom joint where the leaves join the stem and strip **off** the leaves at the first joint up. Now keep the leaves **on** at the next joint, then **remove** the leaves at the next joint, and so on to the top of the stem. Snip diagonally at each joint where you removed leaves. Be sure to keep the cuttings the right way up - each length will yield several of these.

Our illustrations show how to deal with the *top* cutting, but all the others are just the same!

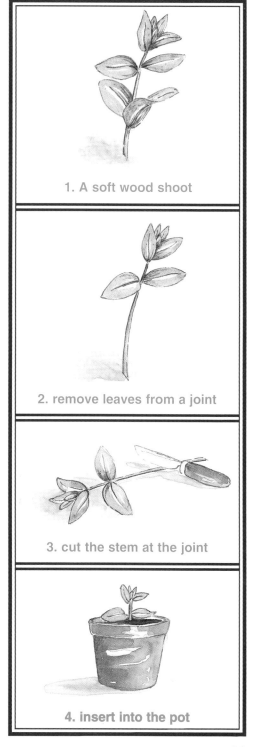

1. A soft wood shoot

2. remove leaves from a joint

3. cut the stem at the joint

4. insert into the pot

25

For each cutting, dip the base in **rooting hormone** to encourage growth and inhibit fungal activity. *Powders* are available, but *hormone rooting fluid* is probably a better option. Then insert the cutting into a pot with the middle (leaved) joint just above the surface of a damp mixture of 1/3 sharp sand, 1/3 peat and 1/3 loam. Three or four cuttings can probably be spaced round the pot, but don't overcrowd them. Cover the pot with a polythene bag which has small ventilation slits cut in it. Ensure that the leaves of your cuttings are not in direct contact with the polythene, as this will render them liable to rotting.

Although the compost should never be *wet*, the atmosphere around the leaves should always be *damp*, so that the condensation from the bag will keep the compost moist. If the pot starts to dry out, don't remove the cover. Instead, stand the pot in a saucer of water for twenty minutes. Place your covered pot in a well lit spot but out of direct sunlight and your cuttings should grow into well-rooted young plants in between three and eight weeks, with speed and success depending on the species you use.

With the smaller shrubby herbs like *thyme*, take cuttings in a similar way. Cut off the top 6cm of a young shoot and remove lower leaves to about halfway. Now dip in rooting hormone and insert into a pot.

Have everything prepared *before* you take your cuttings, and try to do it on a shady day. Your chances of success will be increased if the cuttings are not allowed to wilt before and during preparation. Take quite a few cuttings to allow for some losses, and work fast!

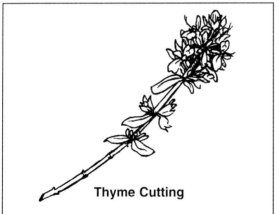

Thyme Cutting

People become very good at cuttings and offer them to their friends with the result that a plant given to you may be five steps removed from its original home and label. In this way herbs often become mis-identified so don't take the name of a gift at its face value. Take care before you eat your new herb - mis-identified plants have been known to kill!

Provençal Mix

In classic cookery *Provençal* simply describes a mixture of *tomatoes* and *garlic*. Herbes Provençales is a meaningless term seen on imported jars of amorphous dried herbs in trendy shops. The herbs may have been actually grown in Provence and may contain any of the following: *rosemary, sweet marjoram, thyme* and a little *sage, lavender* and *orange* zest. But then again they may not. Better to play safe and make your own.

6. | *Design your own herb garden*

Here are some lists of popular herbs which will help you design your own herb beds, and perhaps also adapt one of the **theme** herb gardens or beds which we feature in the next chapter. Many of the herbs are featured in the *picture boxes* throughout the book, and others have notes about them in *chapter 10.*

Hemlock

Some plants have a variety of uses and can appear in several beds. Other plants - *hemlock* for instance - are so readily confused with culinary herbs that they are best left out of the garden altogether. Even if you don`t plant them yourself, seeds may blow over and germinate with disastrous consequences.

Much media attention has been devoted to **poisonous** herbs, but only a small proportion of plants are dangerous and none is recommended in this chapter. However some people can react in wholly unexpected ways to plants and caution is always advisable until you are familiar with handling and eating them. *Rue* is particularly liable to cause a skin reaction and although a very attractive plant and one regarded as essential in Renaissance physic gardens, it should be avoided by children and people with sensitive skins.

Rue

It is a sound generalisation that most plants hate empty spaces and in practical terms an isolated plant is the obvious target for predators to home in on. It will have no shelter from the wind and any bindweed left in the soil will invariably try and climb it. From this has grown up the doctrine of **companion planting** though when put to the test, most plant associations seem to be based on a mixture of coincidence and wishful thinking. Some plants are also believed to be hostile to others, most famously *rue*, though I have never seen it growing in isolation in a herb garden. That said, plants can release chemicals in the soil, the mechanisms of which are not fully understood, either for protection or to prevent competition from the same species.

For instance *roses* are very rarely successful where other roses have grown before. On the other hand, a gardening saying which does seem genuinely to work is that "*garlic* is good for roses". Whether this is because the sulphur involved in the garlic's metabolism increases the rose's resistance to fungoid diseases or whether the bulbs exude something that increases the scent of the roses is not clear, but it is certainly worth trying, Another experiment with an above average success rate is to grow *camomile* alongside any plant that looks sickly. It is said to be a sure-fire way of cheering the wilted.

Sweet Marjoram

Grow as an annual from seed, sowing in trays indoors (heated). Sow outdoors only from May. Needs full sun, light soil and regular watering. One of several varieties of *marjoram,* this is similar to *pot marjoram,* but the flavour is entirely different. It possesses a gentle warmth which can deliciously permeate an entire dish, but can easily be cooked out, so it is best (like all *soft* herbs) with lightly cooked food. Not very pleasant with fish. Also used as a herb tea, and to attract bees and butterflies to the garden.

12. Sweet Marjoram
(Origanum majorana)

I start with a selection of perennial **culinary herbs** as these are the most popular. They also form fixed points in the herb garden amongst which the annuals can be sown. Leave plenty of room for expansion between them and fill in the gaps with *dill, chervil* and other suggestions from the following section.

Perennial culinary herbs	
These are suitable for an English herb bed, appreciating rich soil and regular watering. Those listed first are not so fussy about light levels as the Mediterranean herbs below.	
Non-fussy perennials:	
Bay	page 6
Chives	page 14
Horseradish	
Lemon Balm	page 45
Lovage	page 46
Mint	page 29
Sorrel	page 40
Sweet Cicely	page 47
Mediterranean perennials:	
Fennel	page 45
Hyssop	page 45
Oregano	page 46
Rosemary	page 35
Sage	page 38
Tarragon	page 41
Thyme	page 46
Winter Savory	

Note:- Page *indicates where the herb is featured.*

Annual and biennial culinary herbs

Annual herbs are those which last a season or less in the garden. They travel and transplant reluctantly and are best raised from seed, either sown in modules as described earlier or directly into the ground. They can either be grown in rows or used as filling between clumps of perennial herbs. Several go to seed themselves very quickly and a succession of summer sowings is required to maintain a constant supply for your kitchen. **Biennial** herbs (marked **B** in our table) seed and die off in their second year.

Annual culinary herbs	
Angelica **B**	page 45
Basil	page 1
Borage	page 9
Chervil	page 45
Coriander	page 19
Dill	page 20
Marjoram, Sweet	page 28
Parsley **B**	page 34
Purslane	page 46
Salad Rocket	page 47
Shiso Perilla	page 47

Note:- page indicates where the herb is featured.

Many of these plants look similar to wild cousins, but don't be tempted to sample the ones you find growing in the hedgerows. Some like *fools parsley* (Aethusa) for instance, are poisonous. Play safe and get your plants and seed from a reputable company.

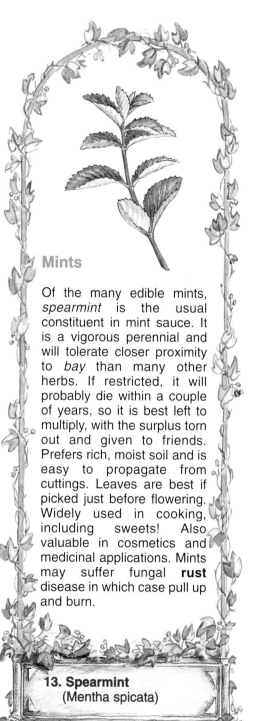

Mints

Of the many edible mints, *spearmint* is the usual constituent in mint sauce. It is a vigorous perennial and will tolerate closer proximity to *bay* than many other herbs. If restricted, it will probably die within a couple of years, so it is best left to multiply, with the surplus torn out and given to friends. Prefers rich, moist soil and is easy to propagate from cuttings. Leaves are best if picked just before flowering. Widely used in cooking, including sweets! Also valuable in cosmetics and medicinal applications. Mints may suffer fungal **rust** disease in which case pull up and burn.

13. Spearmint
(Mentha spicata)

Extending your choice

Although most people start with the basic culinary herbs, their enthusiasm soon gets the better of them, especially after seeing the range available either in a glossy book or during a visit to a specialist nursery. The more they cram in, the more their herb garden becomes interesting rather than being simply utilitarian. Under these circumstances, there will be a certain amount of jostling for position among the plants so don't be inhibited about moving those that don't seem to be flourishing to a new position or even giving way to your addiction and creating a whole new bed for them.

Fortunately many herbs do not take up much space but **how tall?** is a question that is usually asked at this point and is always difficult to answer. So much depends on the weather, the soil and yourself. A herb that you enjoy eating every week is never going to get as big as one whose flavour you detest. However some herbs never grow tall but, like *thyme* for instance, stay short and spread sideways. Others, such as *lovage*, that depend on the wind to scatter their seeds can reach several feet. When planning a garden it is easiest just to divide them in to tall, medium and short - here is our selection.

Tall herbs (over 130cm)

Angelica   page 45
Artichoke
Bay   page 6
California bay*, juniper and other trees
Black Cohosh
Collinsonia   *Some people are
Colquhounia   dangerously
Elecampane   allergic to this.
Elsholtzia
Fennel   page 45
Joe Pye and other eupatiorums
Lemon Verbena   page 24
Lovage   page 46
Mallows
Mullein
Purple Loosestrife
Russian Tarragon   page 41
(useless as a herb, use it as a vegetable)

Medium herbs

Some artemisias
Euphorbias
Lavenders   page 21
Rosemarys   page 35
Sages   page 38

Short herbs

Many artemisias
Most labiates i.e. thymes (page 46), mints
(page 29), Marjorams (page 28) etc.
Many alliums
Basil (outdoor)   page 1
Coriander   page 19
Saffron
Violets

Some edging plants

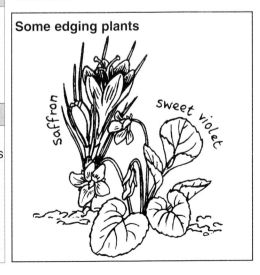

saffron

sweet violet

7.	*Theme gardens*

Theme gardens are always popular and provide an interesting talking point. They might be linked to the occupation of the owner: a doctor could have an apothecary's garden and a historian a medieval garden. Here we look briefly at some themes that you might use as a basis for your own herb garden design, together with comments on which herbs suit particular garden positions and soil types.

Damp and shady garden

Sadly the number of culinary herbs that will grow in damp shady conditions is limited. *Cranberries* will grow in acidic damp sand, as will *cowslips* for wine and salads, *bistort*, the essential ingredient of the "dock pudding" celebrated in Northern industrial towns and *sweet gale*, traditional in home brews in both England and Germany. However because children are normally kept away from streams, it is possible to plant some attractive and interesting medicinal plants in this area which should **not** be eaten. Amongst these are the *loosestrifes*, both yellow and purple, *valerian, bethroot, Joe Pye, twinleaf, turtle blooms* and *poke root.* All should be planted just above the water line.

The roman garden

As well as an aid to history education, the design shown on page 32 makes an ideal sun trap and a D.I.Y. enthusiast could easily make an impressive reproduction Roman pavilion. Failing that, persuade the set designer from the local dramatic society to build a *Roman* facade on to an ordinary summer house. The design should be open and airy to let in the sun and all the scents of the garden.

At home, the Romans lived in a hot climate with no refrigeration and so meat and game were spiced to an extent that we would find unpalatable today. One favourite was *silphium* thought to be a particularly potent strain of the plant known today as *devil's dung* or *asafoetida*. Ordinary *asafoetida* is readily obtainable today and is used in the preparation of curries and many Middle Eastern dishes. Roman food was frequently cooked in heavily reduced wine that had been flavoured with *elecampane, roses, wormwood* and *violets*. Honey was used to counter the sour taste of many of the vinegar and rancid wine-based preservatives and so our plan includes a bee hive. Because of the heat of a Roman summer, water was important, though fountains were usually limited to the villas of the patrician classes. All the perennial plants suggested should survive an English winter.

Roman Garden

The pavilion is a double cube, and the pond and paving are rectangles with with length twice their width.

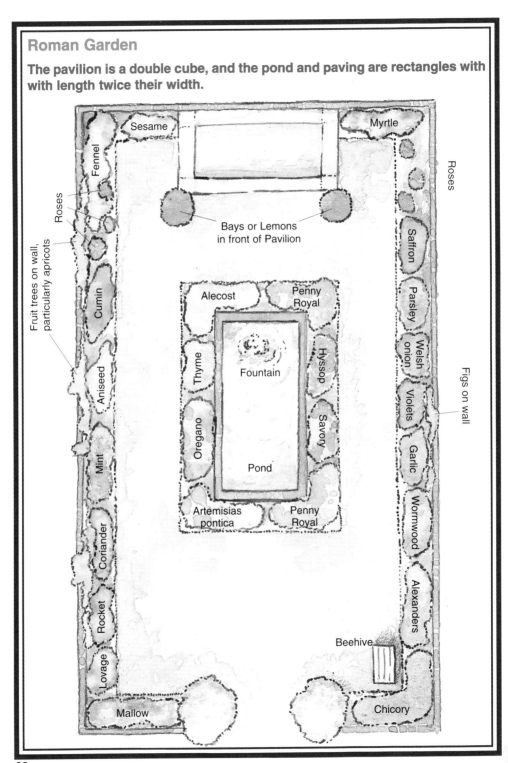

Sesame

Myrtle

Fennel

Roses

Roses

Bays or Lemons
in front of Pavilion

Fruit trees on wall,
particularly apricots

Saffron

Cumin

Alecost

Penny
Royal

Parsley

Aniseed

Thyme

Fountain

Hyssop

Welsh onion

Oregano

Savory

Violets

Mint

Pond

Garlic

Figs on wall

Artemisias
pontica

Penny
Royal

Wormwood

Coriander

Alexanders

Rocket

Lovage

Beehive

Mallow

Chicory

A dyer's garden

Many people expect more from their herb garden than just some ways to make their food more interesting. Often they turn to dyeing fabric. This is a vast and specialist subject, which is best investigated in your local library. In the meantime, here are some suggestions to get you started, with *woad* featured on page 47 as a particularly popular dye herb.

Herb	Part Used	Colour
Agrimony	leaves	yellow
Alder Buckthorn	bark	brown
"	berries	sap green
Alkanet	roots	red
Allium bulbs	bulb skins	gold
Barberry	leaves	black
"	roots	yellow
"	twigs	red/yellow
Bearberry	all	blue/green
Black Elder	berries	violet
"	leaves	lemon
Bloodroot	roots	red
Coltsfoot	all	green
Dyers Camomile	Flowers	gold
Ceanothus americanus	roots	red
Dyers Greenweed	Tips	yellow/green
Elecampane	roots	blue
False Indigo	leaves	indigo
Gipsywort	all	black
Goldenrod	flowers	yellow/bronze
Hollyhock	flowers	blue
Juniper	berries	brown
Ladys Bedstraw	Roots	red
"	shoots	yellow
Ladys Mantle	Green parts	green
Larkspur	flowers	green
Lily of the Valley	leaves (Spring)	yellow/green
"	leaves (Autumn)	gold
Madder	roots	red
Mares Tails	Plant but not stems	Chrome
Marjoram	all	reddish
Marigold (calendula)	flowers	creamy yellow
Meadowsweet	Shoots	green/yellow
"	roots	black
"	leaves	blue
Motherwort	all	dark green
Nettle	all	green
Orris	crushed flower juice	green
Parsley	leaves	green
Pokeweed	berries	red
Saffron	stigmas	yellow
St Johns Wort	tops	yellow
Sassafras	flowers	yellow
Sorrel	leaves	green/yellow
Sumac (Rhus glabra)	berries	yellow
"	dry leaves	tan
Tansy	leaves	yellow/green
Virginia Creeper	berries	pink
Woad	leaves	blue

flat leaf

curled

Parsley

Everyone knows *parsley,* a biennial usually grown as an annual from seed, which should be as fresh as possible. Widely used in cooking, with leaves best picked fresh as required, *parsley* contains an enormous range of vitamins and trace elements necessary to maintain health and in return requires rich ground to grow in. The three most familiar types are *curled, flat leaf* (or *French*) and *Hamburg.* The latter is grown for its roots and is traditional in some Jewish dishes. Some people are allergic to *parsley* and may develop a rash if they handle the herb on a hot day.

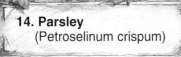

14. Parsley
(Petroselinum crispum)

Herbs on a north facing wall

One of the most difficult sites to deal with is a North facing wall with only a narrow bed in front of it. Because most culinary herbs need the warmth and light of full sun to develop their flavour and scent, your range of choice is limited. The good news is that you can grow plants up against it that would blow over in more open conditions (for example *angelica* and *lovage*). Also the wall could be a positive advantage in confining herbs that might otherwise become rampant (like *horseradish* and most kinds of *mint*). Many of the taller herbs are comparatively plain, so *variegated ivies* and *roses* should be encouraged to climb the wall. Amongst the most suitable roses are **Mme Alfred Carrière, Zephirine Drouhan, Gloire de Dijon** and **Alberic Barbier**, which will need supporting with wall ties. *Ivy* berries are a great attraction for the birds in your garden but no part of the plant should be eaten by humans. *Rose* petals on the other hand are the main constituent of rose petal jam and essential in rose water and many Eastern dishes.

Hollyhocks are another edible plant that could provide a flash of colour for what might otherwise be rather a gloomy situation, but if you use these, remember that regular watering is essential to prevent rust on the leaves. If you are tempted to use *aconites* and *delphiniums* on the basis that they have been used as medicinal herbs, bear in mind that they are very poisonous. This site could also usefully house a few *juniper* bushes. You need both sexes to get any berries and they take several years to mature sufficiently to set fruit but they are worth waiting for, being delicious crushed in to a paste and served as a sauce not just with game but with many brassicas too.

Bergamot is one brightly flowered perennial herb that could be planted in this bed. Other useful herbs include *chives, claytonia, sweet cicely* and *sorrel.* Using these plants above as a foundation fill in the bare ground around them with short lived herbs grown from seed like *chervil, dill* and *parsley.*

Herbs on a south facing wall

South facing walls provide wonderful opportunities - they bounce the heat off the brickwork and are less inclined to dry out at the base than those which face north and east. The temptation is to grow fruit up them, but *jasmines* will do well as will many passion flowers, some varieties of which set fruit and others of which are used in medicine. At the back plant *lemon verbena* and the *elsholtzias.* These latter, which should not be confused with a similarly named poppy, are usually tall shrubby plants and although related to *thymes* and *sages,* are totally useless in the kitchen. Their redeeming feature is an amazing bathroom like fragrance. Grow them as an unusual scented talking point.

Most herbs will grow in this situation: *rosemarys, thymes, lavenders, oreganos, savories, hyssops, tarragon* and *calamints.* Most of these will only release their scent either on hot

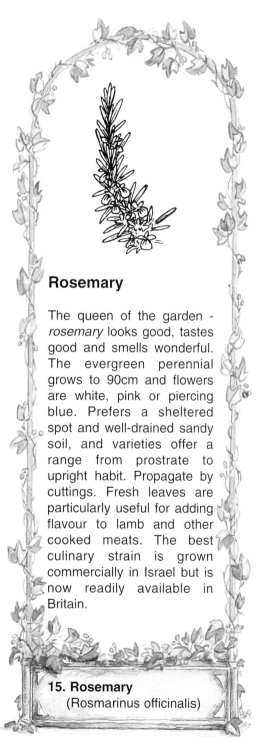

Rosemary

The queen of the garden - *rosemary* looks good, tastes good and smells wonderful. The evergreen perennial grows to 90cm and flowers are white, pink or piercing blue. Prefers a sheltered spot and well-drained sandy soil, and varieties offer a range from prostrate to upright habit. Propagate by cuttings. Fresh leaves are particularly useful for adding flavour to lamb and other cooked meats. The best culinary strain is grown commercially in Israel but is now readily available in Britain.

15. Rosemary
(Rosmarinus officinalis)

afternoons or if crushed but if you scatter *coriander* seed about their roots, you will find this herb will scent the evening air without assistance. *Basil* is never really reliable outside, but if you want to try, this is the place for it.

Island beds have the advantage that you can get at them from all sides, but the disadvantage that you can not easily reach the middle, so plant something large in the centre that you won't want too often like a *bay tree* surrounded by a huge clump of *lavender. Elecampane, woad* and bronze *fennel* are also good for the middle, providing a contrast of leaf shape and colour. For those with time on their hands, the bed could be edged with box, which in the initial stages will need constant weeding, or with *Nepeta nervosa* or *N grandiflora*. Another idea is to plant *mint* on the edge where it will be easy to tear out if it gets too invasive.

High beds, unlike raised beds are structures built to waist level or even higher. They are ideal for the disabled gardener and for introducing low growing plants to the partially sighted. Because they are well drained, they are specially suited for growing *thymes, oregano* and *savory*. Try contrasting golden *marjoram* with the purple *clover, Trifolium repens purpurescens. Clover* is used in soups and salads in Scandinavia, but is rarely used in Britain perhaps because of its reputation for causing infertility in sheep and thrush in horses.

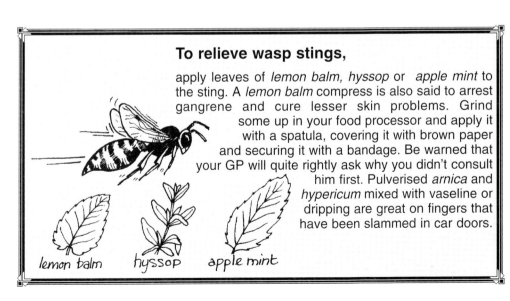

To relieve wasp stings,

apply leaves of *lemon balm, hyssop* or *apple mint* to the sting. A *lemon balm* compress is also said to arrest gangrene and cure lesser skin problems. Grind some up in your food processor and apply it with a spatula, covering it with brown paper and securing it with a bandage. Be warned that your GP will quite rightly ask why you didn't consult him first. Pulverised *arnica* and *hypericum* mixed with vaseline or dripping are great on fingers that have been slammed in car doors.

lemon balm   hyssop   apple mint

Herb bog garden

Few houses are built on acidic boggy ground, but you might be unlucky. It has to be admitted that the best culinary herbs hate these conditions, but it is possible to establish a herb garden nevertheless. Moreover given the unusual terrain, you will be able to grow plants less commonly seen in more orthodox herb gardens. *Star anise, skunk cabbage, labrador tea* and many other traditional North American medicinal plants come to mind. Other herbs can still be grown, but they will have to be cultivated under the conditions described for patio plants. If you live in the drier parts of the country, you will have to create your own swamp. This is easily done by excavating a pond about a foot deep, lining it with

Wiping a clove of garlic

around a salad bowl is for wimps, as is using a *garlic* crusher. Spanish peasants put the entire bulb on the stone floor and stamp on it. The individual cloves separate easily and can be removed from the skin with no problems. Throw the whole lot in the salad or cassoulet.

Mediterranean people claim the following methods are the best ways of avoiding garlic smells on the breath.

(1) Always use *garlic* with *parsley.*

(2) Drink lots of coarse red wine with the meal.

(3) Make love to a lusty Provençal peasant immediately afterwards. This is not recommended: allow at least two hours after eating to digest the meal and avoid the risk of heart failure.

polythene in the usual way, then filling it completely with a mixture of peat, top soil and sand. If it is constructed on a slope, gradations of **bogginess** can be incorporated so that plants that like damp as opposed to semi-aquatic conditions can be grown.

Patio herb garden

You might love herbs but hate gardening, in which case a patio garden is the answer. Go out and

Sage

Likes full sun and light, well drained alkaline soil. Grow from seed or cuttings, then prune after flowering and plant should last for five years or so, reaching 60cm. Leaves are best picked just before flowering starts. Many varieties including *Balkan sage (S. fruticosa),* the best to cook with, and *red sage,* often used in sausages. The herb was venerated in medieval China. *Clary sage (S. sclarea)* is grown on a massive scale in USA for the perfumery trade: grow some and add a sprig to your bath for a wonderful perfume and relaxation.

choose some nice paving and put all your favourite herbs in large troughs and pots. The advantages of this kind of garden are that it allows you to move plants around in infinite permutations to suit you best and also, because you can bring your plants in during the winter, you can grow herbs that would otherwise not normally survive in an English garden. *Elsholtzias, daturas, pelargoniums, lemon verbena* and the subtropical *lavenders* all add a touch of the exotic. Do remember though that pots full of compost are very heavy to wheel around and those not equipped with handles may require sack trucks. Sack trucks themselves will not go up steps so if your patio is terraced, remember to have ramps as well as steps.

Another important point to remember is that although you only get out what you put in, some plants are far greedier than others. *Parsley* and *chives* are notoriously hungry so if you have a trough of them near your barbecue and you keep picking them, they will quickly become exhausted unless you remember to feed them. Other plants like *mint* move on the fresh ground by means of runners. If they are confined they will choke themselves to death within a year, so always remember to start your *mint* pot every spring with fresh compost and the few healthiest runners from the previous season. A final tip when building your patio is to remember to install a **garden tap** before laying the cement. People can be extremely tetchy about hoses run from the kitchen tap!

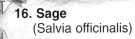

16. Sage
(Salvia officinalis)

8.	*Autumn and winter*

Herb gardens have a reputation for being deadly dull places in winter but you can console yourself with the fact that the herb gardener's winter is an extraordinarily short season which never leaves sufficient time to do all the jobs you wanted to do. However, herb gardens can be depressing if insufficient care was taken in preparing the plants for what should be their season of rest and consolidation.

As winter approaches, **prune** off all brown and surplus foliage so there will be no rotting remains to be seen on your herbs. Compost or burn the clippings to avoid problems caused by parasites and fungus. Cut back **perennials** like *lovage* and *elecampane* to the ground. You will probably see next year's shoots already forming on the *elecampane* when you do this. *Fennel* too should be cut right back and the **sticks** collected on a dry day and stored in the larder, hanging in bunches from the ceiling. The last traces of the **annuals** should be dug out and composted though you may find that *chervil* has already self-seeded and so may be left to continue growing through the winter. *Horseradish* will have died back, but can still be dug up to provide a fresh herb flavour for mackerel and roast beef.

If some clumps have become too large, they can be dug up and **split** in late autumn. Try to keep the soil/root ball together while digging it up. Then with a pair of forks pushed into the clump from above, lever into two pieces. Repeat until your new pieces are the size you want, then re-plant. This process is a useful way of getting new plants and works well for *chives, comfrey, mint* and *tarragon*.

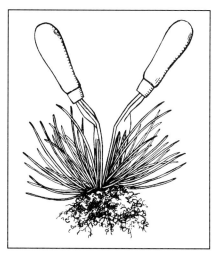

In a warm season, *rosemary* may start flowering just before Christmas and the *witch hazel* shortly after, so that in an exceptional year, you may have continuous flowering from late summer to early spring. From *bergamots* and *lavender* "Grappenhall" through *colchicum*, *rosemary*, and *witch hazel* to the North American spring flowering medicinals like *sanguinaria* and *jeffersonia* - with care and planning you are seldom without colour!

(Note: colchicum or wild saffron is a poisonous medicinal herb and should not be eaten).

Some plants - like *bays, rosemarys* and *lavenders* - will keep their leaves all winter just like a *box* hedge. Mediterranean plants like *tarragon* should be protected from winter weather, perhaps using bracken or straw but only if stuffed in polythene bags.

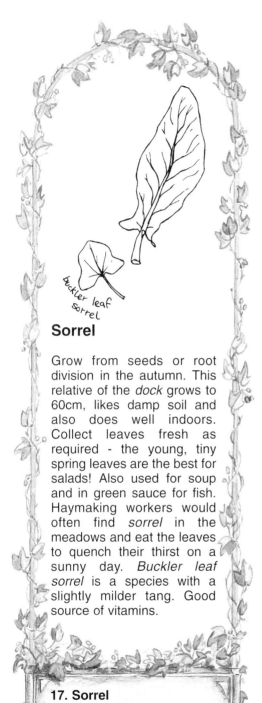

Sorrel

Grow from seeds or root division in the autumn. This relative of the *dock* grows to 60cm, likes damp soil and also does well indoors. Collect leaves fresh as required - the young, tiny spring leaves are the best for salads! Also used for soup and in green sauce for fish. Haymaking workers would often find *sorrel* in the meadows and eat the leaves to quench their thirst on a sunny day. *Buckler leaf sorrel* is a species with a slightly milder tang. Good source of vitamins.

17. Sorrel
(Rumex acetosa)

If it gets wet, straw spreads disease to rot your plants, and also prevents you from seeing when the plants are shooting again in the spring. I recommend **cloches** in rows or large upturned frost-resistant terra cotta pots to cover individual plants. Larger specimens like *myrtles* and tender young *bays* were traditionally sheltered by bee skeps, but these days the bubble film used for packaging may be easier to purchase.

Preserving Herbs

In between autumn and spring you can avoid buying expensive fresh herbs from the supermarket by using your own preserved herbs. The part of the herb that provides its scent and flavour is a volatile oil stored in the plant cells. Strong light and temperature above about 30°C will cause the oil to escape leaving nothing except some brownish twigs.

Freeze drying works best. Collect your herbs immediately before flowering on a warm morning as soon as the dew has evaporated. Bring them in to the kitchen in a covered basket, strip off the leaves and discard any bugs. Put the leaves on a tray in the deep freeze until they are just crisp, which normally takes about 30 minutes. Then place in a very cool oven with the door open for about five minutes. Remove and tightly stopper in a dark jar - most coffee jars stored in an unlit cupboard are ideal. Obviously freezers, ovens and kitchen draughts vary, so you might have to try this a few times before you work out your winning formula.

Another method is to take leaves and chop them finely. Single herbs or a mixture of (for example) *sage, marjoram, thyme* and *parsley* are suitable. Then put a good pinch into each of the sections of an **ice-cube** tray. Top up with water and freeze.

When the cubes are frozen, remove them in the usual way and store them in the freezer in polythene bags. They should last for several months and are ideal for cooking or adding to cold drinks.

Hanging herbs from the clothes line over the Aga has become fashionable. It is a ridiculous idea. The herbs are exposed to variations in temperature, the kitchen lights, other cooking smells and dirt. They are also a favourite target for hibernating wasps. Bundles hung in an airing cupboard or attic might be worth trying, but freezing is to be preferred!

Herbs can also be stored as **preserves.** Mint sauce and horse radish are two of the most familiar. *Basil*, the herb which least lends itself to drying, can either be stored as **pesto** or packed tightly in a jar of virgin olive oil. At the end of the year both the leaves and the oil will be black and evil looking but the basil will taste more like *basil* than the dried product and the oil will form the basis of a superb dressing. (This has apparently been banned from sale in USA recently.) Commercial products are no substitute for the enjoyment to be derived from growing and preserving your own herbs.

basil leaves

Pesto is made by pounding fresh *basil* leaves in olive oil and mixing the pulp with *garlic,* pine kernels, parmesan and sardo cheeses.

Tarragon

Shrubby perennial that likes rich, dry light soil and a sunny but sheltered site. Reaches 1m and is only grown from cuttings or root division, both in spring. Grow without using fertilisers, and keep dry in winter to avoid rot. Used in sauce Béarnaise and in vinegar. Two main varieties of "the little dragon" are commonly available. *French tarragon* is the one used in cooking, and is grown from cuttings or root division. *Russian tarragon* comes from seed, and is mainly of use as a horse feedstuff, mixed with hay, so **read the label** and **sniff** before purchase!

18. Tarragon
(Artemisia dracunculus)

9.	*Some final jottings*

Herbs may be mainly used for food flavouring, but they have lots of other uses. A principal one these days is to provide pleasure in a garden - many a fine herb is grown and enjoyed, but never eaten! This book has concentrated on choosing and growing herbs, but I will just touch on some of their other roles in our lives.

Medicinal Herbs
Sooner or later everyone with a herb garden, usually when suffering from flu or a hangover, wants to maximize its use by growing **medicinal** herbs. It cannot be over emphasised that if you are sick, go and consult your GP. That said, some people, whether from fear, past bad experiences or on religious grounds will refuse to do so and are left with self-treatment as the only remedy available to them. For these and with a National Health Service over burdened by the treatment of minor complaints, the domestic cultivation of medicinal herbs has to be an interesting idea, particularly when some traditional preparations are becoming difficult to obtain.

However the idea that herbs are slow acting with no side effects is a fallacy which could easily prove fatal. *Feverfew* is excellent for headaches but can cause dermatitis. *Comfrey* was used for centuries in the treatment of broken bones and strained limbs but has now been linked with cancer as has *borage* which is supposed to alleviate hangovers. *Valerian* is one of the best natural tranquillizers but is thought to cause varying but unspecified side effects.

If you want to **treat yourself**, buy your plants from a herb expert, say what you want the plants for and ask his advice, then read at least four different books on the problem - you need to do this as too many books are guilty of copying one anothers errors. Never take more than a quarter of the recommended dose until you are certain that you are not allergic to the plants' constituents. Only then start gradually increasing your intake. To be truly certain, there are some reputable short courses in herbal medicine available. They are worth taking for general interest even if you don`t want to be a fully fledged herbalist.

A pelargonium leaf
at the bottom of a baking tin will deliciously suffuse into a sponge cake. The flavours available include chocolate, strawberry, roses, citrus and peppermint.

The Birds And The Bees

Herb gardens can be as beneficial to **wild life** as to humans and an interesting informal or wild garden can be created for this purpose. The easiest way of accomplishing this is to remove several patches of turf and plant a clump of (say) half a dozen wild flowers of a single variety out of 8cm pots in each space. Choose species which have a role in feeding birds, butterflies and moths present in your area - either as nectar plants or as food plants for the caterpillars.

From these nucleus colonies, the wild flowers will soon start to spread out without further help. Although this is a largely low maintenance concept, it is essential not to allow one species of plant to become dominant. This is best accomplished by cutting the heads off the over-vigorous species before they set seed. In any case mow the whole plot at the end of summer. Many caterpillar food plants are also traditional human medicinal herbs. Research has increasingly shown that chemicals found in these plants are frequently incorporated by caterpillars into natural defence systems against predators.

Bees will be frequent visitors to your herb garden. Along with other insects, they are particularly drawn by *borage, mint, chives, hyssop, rosemary* and *lavender*.

Small **nectar** plants you might consider will include *ageratum, Bergenia crassifolia, betony, bluebell, calamint, coltsfoot, forget-me-not, lucerne, marjoram, primrose, thrift, thyme, tormentil* and *yarrow*.

Plants for **egg-laying and caterpillar feeding** might include *bird's foot trefoil, cowslip, dogwood, heathers, honesty, red clover, sorrel, stinging nettle* (really important!), *sweet rocket, tormentil, dog & sweet violet*.

Which plants you choose to include will depend on space available, on the aspect and soil type, and on the preferences of the animals you want to attract. This needs some planning of course, but help is available in our companion title *Your Butterfly Garden* (see **Appendix**).

Potagers

Potagers are the link between herb and vegetable gardens. The six classical potager herbs are *orach, spinach, lettuce, sorrel, sea kale beet* and *purslane. Dandelion, rocket* and *good King Henry* can be added to the list. One might also plant many of the newly available Chinese vegetables, most of which are very decorative.

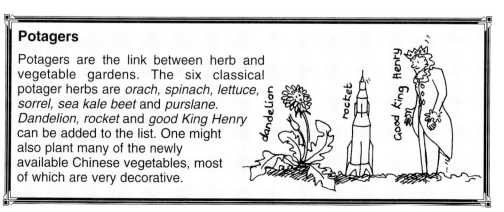

periwinkle

Herbs as ground cover

Several herbs make cheap and effective ground cover which provides a variety of foliage and a pretty cover of flowers in season. *Camomile* is now famous as an alternative lawn, but it needs almost continuous weeding in its first year. After this, it makes an aromatic and fairly hard-wearing lawn. Ask for the variety which does not flower, as this means little cutting will be needed. One idea is to make a small square or circle of *camomile* lawn as a feature.

Other herbs which can provide ground cover include *lungwort* and *woodruff* (both good in shade conditions), *marjoram* (a compact variety), *lemon thyme* (creeping, with tiny pink flowers), *periwinkle, Corsican mint* and *pennyroyal*.

Cosmetics

Several herbs are the basis for cosmetics which can be made at home - including *elderflower, camomile* and *comfrey*. Cleansers, face cream and skin toners can all be produced, and details will be found in specialist magazines and books.

potpourri

Potpourri

A decorative and pleasantly scented potpourri can be made using a selection of dried herbs. The actual plants used can be chosen from a wide range, but the basic method is as follows. Put a few drops of an aromatic oil into a mixing bowl (for example clove oil). Put in a selection of dried herb leaves (such as *bay leaves, lemon verbena* and *marjoram*) together with a larger quantity of dried *rose* petals. Mix together, add some ground cinnamon or other spice, then mix again, adding dried flower heads and more scented oil (for example lavender oil) until the mixture looks and smells good. Place in a sealed jar for about five weeks, then use in an open container as a room freshener. A great hobby, and each mix can be different!

And finally

This book will have safely carried you through your first year in the herb garden. It is only a beginning to what may well become a happy addiction. Many herb nurseries carry twenty kinds of *mint*, thirty *thymes* and dozens of varieties of *marjoram*, *rosemary* and *lavender*, offering you endless scope for enlarging your collection beyond the basic essentials mentioned here. You may even find that you like one group of plants so much that you want to start a National Collection.

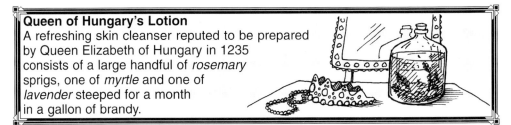

Queen of Hungary's Lotion
A refreshing skin cleanser reputed to be prepared by Queen Elizabeth of Hungary in 1235 consists of a large handful of *rosemary* sprigs, one of *myrtle* and one of *lavender* steeped for a month in a gallon of brandy.

Angelica (Angelica archangelica)

A biennial; use only the freshest seed or you may fail to grow any! Has a beneficial effect on the digestion and is used in several liqueurs and as a flavour for ice cream. Grows to about 2 metres and inclined to blow over, so does best against a wall; see it gets enough water.

Chervil (Anthriscus cerefolium)

Annual, height to 60cm. Traditionally an insignificant herb for omelettes, but recently its subtle liquorice-like flavour has become more appreciated for salads and as a garnish to many other dishes. Delicate, so best used uncooked. It actually dislikes heat and light and flourishes best in spring and autumn, so is a useful filler for difficult parts of the herb garden.

Fennel (Foeniculum vulgare)

Tall (up to 1.5m) and spectacular (especially bronze form) perennial which grows virtually anywhere with good drainage. Protect from slug damage. Roots used as vegetable (Florence variety); leaves are delicious with fish; seeds used in home-made curry powder. Prune to 10cm in autumn.

Hyssop (Hyssopus officinalis)

Attractive mini-shrub with blue, pink or white flowers. Said to have been used by medieval monks to counter effects of excess cholesterol in their diets; very good with fatty foods like goose. Use as an alternative to thyme; pick leaves as flowers first appear; strong flavour. Grows to 60cm and makes good low hedge. Prefers sunny position and light soil.

Lemon Balm (Melissa officinalis)

Hardy perennial reaching 75cm, with strong lemon-scented leaves. Roots are invasive, so confine it to your chosen area. Used in history as a poultice for wounds; try it today by floating leaves in summer drinks; wrap round fish (inside foil) before barbecues; fry with mushrooms; add to fruit before stewing.

Thyme

Strongly scented perennial herb much enjoyed by the Ancient Greeks. Reaches 30cm and prefers full sun and light, well-drained soil. A spreading herb which can be propagated by root division, cuttings and seeds. Prune just before or after flowering, not in autumn. There are 100+ forms, of which the best eating varieties are *common, broad-leaf* and *lemon thyme.* Many culinary uses, including soups, sauces and stuffing mixtures. Also used in cosmetics and as a medicinal herb. Other varieties are used in rockeries, for edging paths and even for sitting on.

19. Thyme
(Thymus vulgaris)

Lovage (Levisticum officinale)

Perennial grows to 2m, with yellowish flowers in the late summer. Likes rich soil and partial shade. Smells strongly of celery and makes a delicious addition to soups and stews (use leaves and seeds sparingly). Used commercially as an ingredient in deodorants.

Oregano (Origanum spp)

Grows well in strong sun, but needs gritty soil to prevent wilting. *Origanum* is the genus name for the various types of *marjoram* which include *sweet marjoram, pot marjoram* and *wild marjoram* (also known as *oregano*). *Greek oregano* has a fiery taste much used in Neapolitan cookery. See also page 28 - *sweet marjoram.*

Purslane (Portulaca oleracea)
A unique appearance resembling a succulent rather than a herb. It is easily grown from seed, provided it is given plenty of warmth and sunlight. If grown indoors, it will self-seed. Little taste or smell but adds a delicious crunchy texture to salads. Can also be cooked like asparagus and served with butter or pickled. Annual, sprawls; height to 15cm.

Salad Rocket (Eruca sativa)

Rocket is a phenomenon of the nineties, seemingly inescapable in salads served throughout the land. Has a delicious nutty flavour that is all its own. Also made into a faux-pesto, substituted for *basil*. The seeds germinate extremely quickly on almost any sunny site, but leaves just as rapidly become coarse and unpleasant so make a new sowing shortly after the first. Grows to 90cm.

Shiso Perilla (Perilla frutescens)

Unusual but increasingly easy to obtain. Has green and purple forms; the purple one is the same colour as opal *basil* and likes the same growing conditions, but has a totally different flavour. Has a curious, but pleasant aroma, grown for pickling in Japan and China and as a meat tenderiser. Used as a bedding plant by Victorian gardeners who were unaware of its culinary advantages. Green form is less attractive but more often eaten fresh by the Chinese.

Sweet Cicely (Myrrhis odorata)

A great favourite - one of the **pudding** herbs, providing a sweet alternative to sugar with a slight aniseed scent. Soft delicate leaves (which can be added to salad or fruit) emerging early in spring, with a mass of frothy white flowers in May. Will self-seed and soon form a large clump, unless the mice eat the seeds first! Perennial eventually reaching 1.5m height.

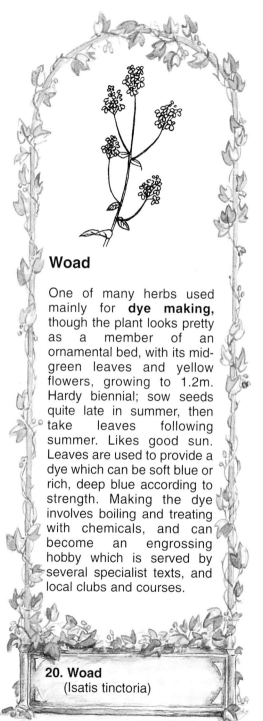

Woad

One of many herbs used mainly for **dye making,** though the plant looks pretty as a member of an ornamental bed, with its mid-green leaves and yellow flowers, growing to 1.2m. Hardy biennial; sow seeds quite late in summer, then take leaves following summer. Likes good sun. Leaves are used to provide a dye which can be soft blue or rich, deep blue according to strength. Making the dye involves boiling and treating with chemicals, and can become an engrossing hobby which is served by several specialist texts, and local clubs and courses.

20. Woad
(Isatis tinctoria)

For further reading, a subjective list of those books I find most useful is given below.

The two most comprehensive books ever published on herb plants are
Modern Herbal   Mrs M Grieve / Peregrine 1976 and subsequent editions.
RHS Encyclopedia of Herbs   Dorling Kindersley 1995

For growing herbs and herb gardens generally
The Herb & Spice Book   Sarah Garland / Frances Lincoln 1979
Herb Gardening   Claire Loewenfeld / Faber 1976

Cooking
Herbs, Spices and Flavourings   Tom Stobart / Penguin 1977
The Herb Book   Boxer and Back / Octopus 1980

Medicinal Herbs
The Herb Book   John Lust / Bantam 1980, strong on dyeing, mythology etc.
The Encyclopedia of Herbs and Herbalism   Malcolm Stuart et al / Macdonald 1986

Herb Garden design
English Herb Gardens   Cooper, Taylor and Bournsell / Wiedenfeld and Nicholson 1986

Commercial growing
Growing Herbs   Rosemary Titterington / Crowood Press 1987

History of Herbs
History of the English Herb Garden   Kay Sanecki / Ward Lock 1992

Aromatic Herbs
Scented Flora of the World   Roy Genders / Hale reprinted 1994

To locate rare plants **The Plant Finder** published annually by the RHS is essential.